Meet the Author

Patricia J. Murphy writes children's storybooks, non-fiction books, early readers, and poetry. She also writes for magazines, corporations, educational publishing companies, and museums. She lives in Northbrook, IL. She especially likes the touch of a cool breeze upon her face and warm sand between her toes.

Your sense of touch can show that you care.

Reading Consultant
Nanci R. Vargus, Ed.D.
Assistant Professor
Literacy Education
University of Indianapolis
Indianapolis, IN

Content Consultant
Beth Cox
Science Learning Specialist
Horry County Schools
Conway, SC

Dedication:
To M.F.H.,
With love, P.J.M.

Library of Congress Cataloging-in-Publication Data

Murphy, Patricia J., 1963–
    Touch / by Patricia J. Murphy.
        p. cm. — (A true book)
    Summary: Explores the sense of touch made possible by the body's largest organ, the skin.
    Includes bibliographical references and index.
    ISBN 0-516-22601-0 (lib. bdg.)   0-516-26972-0 (pbk.)
    1. Touch—Juvenile literature. [1. Touch. 2. Senses and sensation. 3. Skin.] I. Title. II. Series.
QP451 .M87 2003
612.8'8—dc21   2001008384

1 2 3 4 5 6 7 8 9 10 R 12 11 10 09 08 07 06 05 04 03

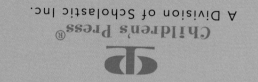

Children's Press®

A Division of Scholastic Inc.

New York Toronto London Auckland Sydney
Mexico City New Delhi Hong Kong
Danbury, Connecticut

A TRUE BOOK™

by
Patricia J. Murphy

TOUCH

Touch is a part of every hour of every day. A ladybug crawls on the back of a girl's hand (right), a less sensitive area for touch.

certain areas of your body are not as sensitive to touch as others are. These areas include the back of your hands, your back, and your arms and legs.

Your sense of touch can be affected by the cold.

When you are out in the cold snow or you sit on your feet, you may not feel your hands or feet. Whether it's freezing temperatures numbing your hands or your body cutting off the

blood to your feet, your receptors cannot send messages. You do not feel a thing!

Other times, people lose their sense of touch because of injuries to their nerve receptors, spinal cord, or the touch center

People who have spinal cord injuries may not be able to feel their feet or legs.

of the brain. These injuries and some diseases stop the brain from getting the nerve impulses or messages.

Sometimes people's brains do not notice certain touches! These touches include the touch of your clothes, shoes, or glasses. If your brain kept feeling these touches, it could not feel new touches. The only time you may feel these touches again is when something changes like you pull up your

After wearing glasses for a while, you may not feel them resting on your nose.

sleeves, untie your shoes, or push up your glasses.

When people cannot feel, they can be in danger. The body's pain receptors warn of injury, illness, and disease. The receptors then tells the body to do something about the pain.

Touch That Helps

Chiropractors and physical therapists use their hands to help people in pain. First, chiropractors find out what causes their pain. Then, they give special treatments with their hands to ease or stop people's pain. One treatment is to move a person's spine in ways to make parts of the body feel better. Physical therapists use massage and movement to treat people with injuries or diseases. They teach people exercises to strengthen or loosen muscles so they can move without pain.

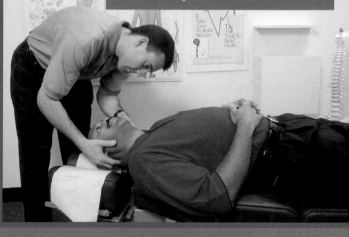

A chiropractor works with a patient.

To become a chiropractor, you must go to a chiropractic college. You must also take a special test to get a license. Then, you can be a chiropractor!

Take Care of Your Skin!

Your skin lets you feel. It protects you and keeps you from harm. You owe it to your skin to protect and take care of it! Here are a few things you can do to keep your sense of touch—and your skin—feeling fine!

• Keep your skin clean. Wash your skin each day. This will

Washing is an important part of taking care of your skin.

help reduce the chance of germs and infection entering your skin. Rub moisturizing lotion on dry skin. Moisturizer will help trap water or moisture that your skin needs. Drink plenty of water to keep your skin moist and healthy.

• Clean cuts with soap and warm water. Apply an antibiotic ointment or cream to kill germs. Place a bandage on your cut. These things will help kill germs that may cause infection. It will also help healing. Seek medical help for deep cuts and burns.

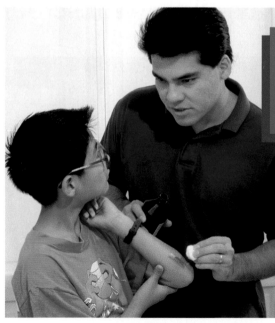

Keeping cuts and scrapes clean and covered will help them heal.

• Do not scrub bug bites, rashes, or poison ivy. Use a hydrocortisone cream. This cream will stop swelling and itching. It will also help stop infection.

• Keep covered up in the sun. Wear light, cotton clothing and wide-brim hats. Apply sunscreen

Wearing a hat with a wide brim will help keep the sun from damaging your scalp and face.

with a sun protection factor (SPF) of 15 and up to uncovered body parts. Stay indoors from 10 A.M. to 2 P.M. when the sun's rays are the strongest. This will help you avoid skin cancer and wrinkles.

• Take care when using sharp or pointy objects like scissors. These objects can hurt your skin and its touch nerve receptors. Do not touch things if you don't know what they are. They could harm you and hurt your skin.

Exercising will keep you and your sense of touch healthy!

• Get plenty of exercise! Exercise keeps blood pumping through your body's blood vessels. This blood carries important nutrients to your skin. It also takes toxins away.

• See a doctor if you notice skin problems. This will keep your skin healthy and problem free!

Facts About Touch

- Your skin covers between 12 to 20 square feet (3.6 to 6.1 square meters) of your body.

- Your skin is about 12 percent of your weight.

- The thickness of your skin is different over your body. Your feet and palms of your hands have the thickest skin! Your eyelids have the thinnest!

- The skin has 3 million sweat glands.

- Your fingerprints are unlike anyone else's.

- Your epidermis sheds thousands of dead skin cells a day.

- You can only see your skin cells under a microscope.

- Newborn babies need touch to live.

- We all need touch to grow and to live.

- Fingernails help your fingers touch objects. Without them, your fingers would just bend upward!

To Find Out More

Here are some additional resources to help you learn more about the sense of touch:

 **Books**

Ballard, Carol. **How Your Body Works: How Do We Feel and Touch?** Raintree Steck-Vaughn, 1998.

Cobb, Vicki. **Feeling Your Way.** Millbrook Press, 2001.

Hurwitz, Sue. **Touch.** Rosen Publishing, 1997.

Moncure, Jane Belk and Viki Woodworth. **My Fingers Are for Touching: My Five Senses.** Child's World, 1998.

Pringle, Laurence. **Explore Your Senses: Touch.** Benchmark Books, 2000.

44

Organizations and Online Sites

Come to Your Senses
*http://tqjunior.
thinkquest.org/3750*

This online site provides
information on your five
senses.

Human Anatomy On-Line
*http://www.innerbody.
com/htm/body.html*

Learn about the human
body.

Neuroscience for Kids
*http://faculty.washington.
edu/chudler/neurok.html*

Learn about all five senses.
Do fun things with your
senses!

Safe Skin
*http://www.sunprotection.
org*

This online site provides
information on how to be
safe in the sun.

Important Words

dermis the inside layer of the skin, it is below the epidermis or outside layer

epidermis the outside layer of the skin

nerve fiber thin long tube that connects nerve receptors to the spinal cord and brain

nerve receptor the end of a nerve where touch, hot/cold, pressure and pain messages are sent to the spinal cord and then to the brain

parietal lobe the part of the brain that involves the senses

somatosensory cortex the area in the brain that receives touch messages

subcutaneous the layer of fat under the skin

thalamus the area of the brain where nerve messages are sorted and put together, they are then sent on to other areas of the brain

Index

(**Boldface** page numbers
   indicate illustrations.)

blind people, 12–13
Braille, Louis, 12–13
chiropractor, 36
dermis, 14, **15,** 17–22, 46
epidermis, 14, **15,** 16, 42,
   46
hot and cold receptor, 20,
   21
injury, 32, 36
nerve fiber, 8, 46
nerve message, 9, 25–26,
   34
nerve receptor, 8, 18–22,
   28, **28,** 30, 32, 41, 46
oil glands, 18
pain receptor, 21–22, 35
parietal lobe, 10, 46

physical therapist, 36
pressure receptor, 20–21
skin
   care, 37–42
   facts, 42
   layers, 7, 14–23
somatosensory cortex,
   9–10, 27, 46
spinal cord, 9, 26–27, 32
subcutaneous, 14, **15,** 23,
   46
sun protection, 16, 40–41
sweat glands, 17, 42
thalamus, 27, 46
touch, purpose of, 7–11
   as protection, 10–11,
   16, 19–22, 35, 40–41
touch receptor, 19–20,
   24–25
vibration, 21

Contents

Your Sense of Touch 5

The Skin You Are In! 14

How Do You Feel? 24

When You Can't Feel 30

Take Care of Your Skin 37

Facts About Touch 43

To Find Out More 44

Important Words 46

Index 47

Meet the Author 48

Your sense of touch lets you know the flower is soft. With your sense of touch, you can feel the hard shell and slimy skin of a snail.

Your Sense of Touch

Go ahead. Reach out and touch a soft, furry, puppy, a silky, smooth, rose, a lumpy, bumpy, rock, or a slippery, slimy worm. These special feelings and thousands of others are brought to you by your sense of touch.

Touch involves your hands, your feet, and your entire body.

While your eyes, ears, nose, and tongue bring your body important information, your sense of touch lets you feel the world around you. Unlike your other four sense organs, your sense of touch is not just in one place. It's all over the place. You touch with your body's largest organ and its largest sense organ—your skin!

Thanks to your skin, you can feel everywhere on your body—from the warmth of a

Some socks feel scratchy when you put them on.

hat on your head to the scratchy, wool socks on your feet. Within the layers of the skin, there are millions of **nerve receptors**, or endings. As these receptors sense touch—or a change in touch—they send special nerve messages or impulses to cells in your body's spinal cord. The spinal cord is a bundle or group of **nerve fibers** that run along your spine. It is connected to your brain.

From your spinal cord, these touch messages travel to the touch center of your brain called the **somatosensory cortex**. The somatosensory cortex is the wide area on the surface of your brain that reaches from one ear to the other. It is located in the **parietal lobe** part of your brain. Once your brain receives these touch messages, you feel!

With the sense of touch, you can learn about the world around you. You can share information with others. You can show your feelings. Touch can also protect your body from harm. Without it, you would

Sometimes friends show how they care by putting an arm around their friends.

not feel a burning, hot stove or a sharp, jagged edge. Pain warns your body that it might be hurt or injured.

The Language of Touch

To read, people who are blind or who have limited sight use books and other documents printed in Braille. Braille is a six-dot system that creates raised marks on paper that the person can feel. The system has sixty-three combinations of raised dots called cells. They include letters, numbers, and punctuation marks.

With her fingers, a blind girl reads a story printed in Braille.

a •	b • •	c • •	d • • •	e • •	f • • •	g • • • •	h • • •	i • •	j • • •
k • •	l • • •	m • • •	n • • •	o • •	p • • • •	q • • • • •	r • • • •	s • •	t • • • •
u • • •	v • • • •	w • • • • •	x • • • •	y • • • • •	z • • • •		**The Braille Alphabet**		

A pattern of dots represents different letters in Braille.

Blinded by an accident as a child, Louis Braille invented Braille to help himself and others learn. He first experimented with a French army captain's twelve-dot night writing system. This helped soldiers read and write in the black of night. Braille's system was easier to use.

Louis Braille

The Skin You Are In!

Your skin has three main layers. They are the **epidermis**, **dermis**, and **subcutaneous**, or fat, layers. Each layer has a different job.

The epidermis acts like a heavy overcoat. It is your body's tough top layer of dead skin cells. The epidermis layer

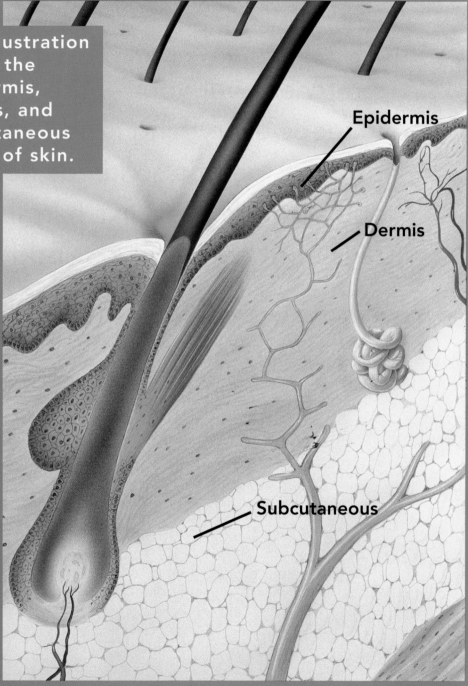

This illustration shows the epidermis, dermis, and subcutaneous layers of skin.

Epidermis

Dermis

Subcutaneous

stretches over your entire body. It keeps everything inside your body inside! It also keeps germs and some of the sun's harmful rays from entering your body.

When you look at your skin, you can see the epidermis layer.

When you are active, the sweat glands in the dermis layer of your skin work to cool you off.

Below the epidermis is the dermis. It is the live layer of skin. This layer is thicker than the epidermis. The dermis's sweat glands cause the body to sweat when it is hot. Its hairs trap warm air when you are cold!

Its oil glands keep the skin waterproof!

The dermis layer also helps your body touch and feel. Within this layer are your body's touch nerve receptors. These receptors come in different

The dermis layer of your skin houses the nerve receptors involved in touching things. For example, these receptors send a message to your brain that the lily pad is smooth.

shapes and sizes. They help your body sense different types of touch and changes in touch. These receptors are touch, hot, cold, pressure, and pain.

• The touch receptors allow you to feel light or soft touch

like the tickle of a feather or a stroke of a finger. Some of them are connected to the roots of your hairs.

• The hot and cold receptors allow the body to sense differences in temperature. They cannot tell how hot the bath water is or how cold the lake will be. They can only tell when the temperature changes!

• The pressure receptors allow you to feel hard touch like a heavy book or a glass falling on your foot. It also lets your

Your skin's hot and cold receptors tell you that the icicle is colder than the winter air.

skin feel fast or slow vibrations like the quick beat of a drum or a soft, summer breeze.

• The pain receptors warn the body when something may cause harm or injury to it, such as a skinned knee or a broken bone. They may also warn your body of illness or disease like a headache or a heart attack. These receptors are found throughout your body.

22

The subcutaneous layer is your body's fat layer. It keeps you warm. It also acts like a shield to protect your body's organs. It provides extra padding when you fall and another layer from the outside world.

Like an extra layer of clothing in winter, the skin's subcutaneous layer helps keep you warm.

How Do You Feel?

All touch starts with a force.
A force is a push or a pull that
gets things moving. Your skin
must be pushed or pulled to
feel touch. For example,
when a hand touches your
shoulder, the touch receptors
are pushed. When someone
grabs your arm, your touch

Your sense of touch starts with a push or a pull.

receptors are pulled. This pulling and pushing triggers your touch receptors.

When someone taps you on your shoulder, the touch receptors in your shoulder send nerve messages or impulses. These

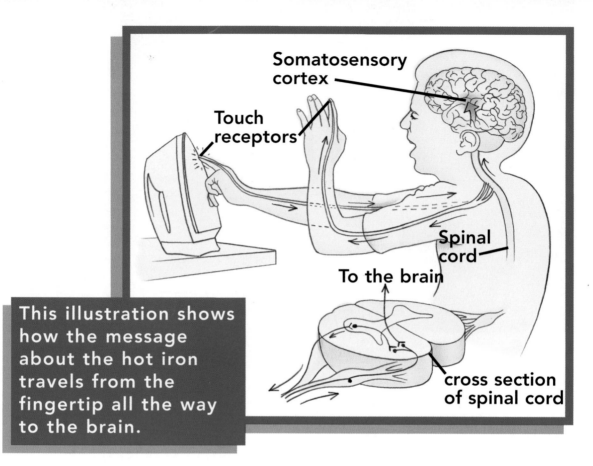

Somatosensory cortex

Touch receptors

Spinal cord

To the brain

cross section of spinal cord

This illustration shows how the message about the hot iron travels from the fingertip all the way to the brain.

nerve messages travel through nerve fibers to nerve cells in the spinal cord. These nerve cells spread the message, "Touch on right shoulder."

These special coded messages travel from the spinal cord to the brain's **thalamus** located in the middle of your brain. This area sorts out the messages, puts them together, and makes sense of them. Next, it sends the messages to a certain "touch" area of the brain's touch center. This center is called the somatosensory cortex. It has different touch areas for each touch area of the body.

The more nerve endings or receptors that a body part has, the larger touch area it has in the brain. The areas on your body that have the most receptors closely packed together are the face, lips, tip of your

tongue, back of your neck, hands, and fingertips. These areas also have the largest "touch" areas in the brain.

Once the messages reach the brain's "touch" center, the brain identifies the touch— "Hey, someone is touching my shoulder!" You feel it. This happens very quickly. In fact, no sooner than you feel a touch, your brain can do something about it. It may tell your body to turn around and say, "Oh, hi Mike!"

When You Can't Feel

You live in a touching and feeling world. It seems like your body is always touching or being touched by something. However, there are some times that the body cannot feel.

Some areas of your body have fewer nerve receptors than others do. As a result,